Old INVERURIE and KEMN

by
Alan Cooper
For Gemma and Karen

George Martin was born at Kinmundy in 1860, the son of a farmer. He carried on the drapery business in High Street for over 50 years from 1887 until his death in 1941 aged 81 years. His interests included collecting guns, breeding and exhibiting Shetland ponies and photography, and he was one of the first amateur photographers in Inverurie. In 1942 the drapery business was bought by J. K. Hay of Inverurie.

© Alan Cooper 2003
First published in the United Kingdom, 2003,
by Stenlake Publishing
Telephone / Fax: 01290 551122
Printed by Cordfall Ltd., Glasgow, G21 2QA

ISBN 1 84033 280 8

The publishers regret that they cannot supply
copies of any pictures featured in this book.

ACKNOWLEDGEMENTS

The publishers would like to thank Robert Grieves for
providing the pictures on pages 2, 14, 15 and the back cover;
W. A. C. Smith for providing the pictures on pages 13, 17 and
43 (lower); and Jimmy Brown for reading the manuscript.

FURTHER READING

The books listed below were used by the author during his research. None of them
are available from Stenlake Publishing. Those interested in finding out more are
advised to contact their local bookshop or reference library.

Brown, Jimmy, *Inverurie Loco Works, The Inside Story*
Burnett, Susan, *Without Fanfare, The Story of my Family*, 1994
Davidson, Revd John, *Inverurie and the Earldom of the Garioch*, 1878
Davidson, Revd John, *Recollections of Forty Years*, 1885
Diack, Hunter, *Boy in a Village*, 1962
Diack, Hunter, *That Village on the Don*, 1965
Downie, Duncan A., *Street Names in the Village of Kemnay*, 1999
Morgan, L. Susan, *The Aberdeenshire Canal, A Study in Transport History*, 1973
Smith, A., *A New History of Aberdeenshire*, Vol. 2
Tawse, H. S. & Allan, G. J., *The Old and New Bridges over the River Don at Inverurie*, 1925
Vallance, H. A., *The Great North of Scotland Railway*, 1965
John Fyfe, One Hundred and Fifty Years, 1846–1996
The Statistical Account of Scotland, 1791–1799, Vol. 14, ed. Sir John Sinclair, 1982
The New Statistical Account of Scotland, Vol. 12, 1845
The Royal Burgh of Inverurie in the Coronation Year, 1902
Banffshire Journal

This photograph of James Easton's Leyland Tiger bus, which
ran from Inverurie to Overton, Monymusk, Cluny Cross Roads
and Kemnay, was taken in the early 1950s in Market Place,
Inverurie, in front of the town hall. The building in the
background on the right with four sets of chimneys is called
Crosslett Court.

INTRODUCTION

Inverurie has its origins in the Earldom of Garioch, which was created in 1160 by King Malcolm IV and conferred by him on his brother, David, Earl of Huntingdon. The earldom included Kintore, Kemnay, Monymusk and Insch, and was administered from castles at Dunnideer and Inverurie (the one at Inverurie was on the Bass). Inverurie is mentioned in documents of the period, with the name appearing as Nrurie, Inrure and Enrowry.

David, Earl of Huntingdon went on the third crusade with Richard the Lionheart and died in 1219, with the earldom eventually passing to his grandson, King Robert I (The Bruce). He bestowed it on his brother-in-law, Gratney, Earl of Mar. It is not known exactly when Inverurie became a royal burgh, although according to tradition it was during the reign of Robert the Bruce. A charter of confirmation was granted in 1558.

In 1696 Inverurie was a very small town with 68 households and only 188 people over the age of sixteen. At the time it had one minister, one teacher and one doctor, with other occupations including weavers (8), tailors (3), smiths (3), shoemakers (7), and merchants (4). There were also 38 domestic servants. The town's population had risen to 162 males and 198 females in 1791, growing rapidly from this period onwards as transport and communications improved and the town became increasingly important as a centre for industry and agriculture.

The Don Bridge was opened in 1791, the toll road to Aberdeen in 1800, the canal in 1805 and the railway line in 1854. When the canal to Aberdeen opened Port Elphinstone consisted of only one house. Inverurie had 93 houses at the time, eleven of which were slated, but aided by the canal and other new transport links both the port and the town grew and flourished. In April 1866 the town council changed the town's name from Inverury to Inverurie to prevent any future confusion in the post offices around the country with Inverary in Argyll, some letters having been sent there by mistake.

The neighbouring settlement of Kemnay existed only as a hamlet until large-scale quarrying commenced in 1858, encouraged by the building of a railway link to the town, with a station opening there in 1859.

THE SQUARE AND LOCOMOTIVE WORKS, INVERURIE FROM THE AIR

The foundation stone of Inverurie's town hall was laid on 10 July 1862. Shops closed at 3 p.m. for the occasion and a procession headed by the volunteer band marched to the Market Place for the ceremony. Within a year the hall had been completed and it was opened on 9 July 1863 with a banquet, dinner and ball attended by 260 people. A band from Aberdeen led by Mr P. Milne played, and the ball went on until 4 a.m. John Russell Mackenzie of Aberdeen was the architect, and the hall cost approximately £3,000 to build. The building to its right opened in May 1880 as a cafe and club called the Inverurie Coffee House for the benefit of young men in the town. This was not a business venture but a philanthropic one funded by Miss Anne Gordon of Manar. Later on it came under the supervision of the YMCA and flourished for many years as the Red Triangle Club. In May 1898 the left part of the building became the post office until this transferred to 23 High Street. The whole building was converted into a fire station in 1940 at a cost of £3,000 (including £1,200 for its purchase), at which point the British Legion, which had been using the upstairs as its local headquarters, moved out and the cafe and tea-rooms on the ground floor were closed.

The fountain in the Market Place was unveiled on 1 November 1879 by Provost Annand as part of events to celebrate the new water supply from the Keith Hall area. Having been turned on by Mrs Annand 'the water rose from the jet at the top, [and] a hearty cheer was given by the crowd assembled' (*Banffshire Journal*, 4 November 1879). The fountain was designed and built by a Mr Keith of Aberdeen, and all the polished parts were made from red Peterhead granite. Its lower basin was seven feet in diameter, and the upper one measured three feet eight inches. In 1956 the fountain was moved by the council but can still be seen at Davah Court where it was re-erected *c*.1972.

John M. Watson (whose shop is in the left foreground of this view) was born in 1833 in Inverurie and on leaving school became an apprentice at Gordon's shoemaker's shop before going on to join the Glasgow engineering firm of Robert Napier & Son. In 1857 he was one of twenty engineers sent by the company to work in India. Having returned to Glasgow he worked on a steamship trading with the Spice Islands in Indonesia. In October 1872 he returned to Inverurie and bought the ironmongery business at 48 Market Place from A. & J. Bisset. He was provost of the town from November 1894 for a year, and died in 1904 aged 71 years. The shop was carried on by his son, James J. Watson, then his grandson, James A. Watson and great-grandson, James S. Watson, who retired in 2000.

44463. J.V.

On the left of this view of the High Street are the Congregational Chapel (foreground, now demolished) and the Masonic Hall. In the background is the spire of what was originally the Methodist Church, opened c.1868. St Anthony's Lodge of Freemasons was founded in 1783 but dissolved c.1837. It reformed with a meeting in the Kintore Arms in October 1872. A newspaper report alludes to over-indulgence in alcohol as being the reason for the break-up of the original group, referring to 'almost a rebellion of the wives of these merry masons' (*Banffshire Journal*, 10 March 1903). The Masonic Hall was opened in December 1881 and altered and extended in 1902, at which point it consisted of a lodge room, retiring room, reading room and two billiard rooms. The architect at the time of the 1902 alterations was George Gray of Inverurie.

In September 1898, following the death of its previous owner, George Murdoch, the Banks of Ury Inn was sold with stables and land attached for £2,150. The new owner was Mr A. Stott, who demolished the buildings and erected a new Banks of Ury Hotel (right, next to the Congregational Chapel). This opened in 1899.

This c.1900 photograph shows North of Scotland Bank manager, Alexander Smith, outside his house. The bank (the small building on the left) opened in 1837. In 1923 the North of Scotland Bank was taken over by the Midland Bank, just four years after the latter had acquired the Clydesdale Bank. Alexander Smith was born at Broomend and educated at Port Elphinstone School and Fordyce Academy. He joined the North of Scotland Bank as an apprentice before being sent to the Oban branch as an accountant and then transferring to Aberdeen. In 1878 he returned to Inverurie as an accountant, becoming the manager there in 1880. Alexander Smith was provost of Inverurie from November 1902 until November 1904, and was an authority on William Thom, the Inverurie poet. He retired in 1925. He had four children: William, an engineer in Glasgow, Alexander, a teacher at Forgue, and two daughters whose married names were Mrs Thomson and Mrs Currie.

The old building at the right-hand edge of this picture had an interesting history. Built at the end of the eighteenth century by the St Anthony's Lodge of Freemasons, it became an inn known as the Mason Lodge Inn. One of its landlords in the early 1800s was George Lyon, chief magistrate of Inverurie and remarkable for his corrupt practices. These included spending the town's income on drink for himself and his friends, as well as imposing fines and selling town property and keeping the money. Revd John Davidson wrote of the later history of the inn as follows: 'The Mason Lodge Inn was owned by Alexander Davidson, who some years later named it the Gordon Arms Hotel, probably in compliment to his wife . . . who had given up that name for his. He had formerly carried on the business of a carpenter or builder, and as dean of guild and treasurer, he held office in the burgh for a long time. After his death, the inn was carried on for a year or two by his daughter and her husband, John Sutherland, painter, and changed hands several times afterwards' (*Recollections of Forty Years*, p24). James Skinner's drapery shop (left) was established in 1847, and Skinner was provost of Inverurie from 1907 until 1922. Both his father, James Skinner, merchant, and father-in-law, William Wyness, butcher, had been provosts in earlier years.

The old Gordon Arms Hotel was bought by John Mann *c.*1880 and after his death was carried on by his widow, Mrs Mann (also known by the name Emily Jackson). She tried to sell the hotel during the years 1899–1901, and at one time the press announced that it had been bought for £5,500, but the deal fell through, possibly because of problems with transferring the licence. Then in 1901 Mrs Mann decided to demolish the hotel and replaced it with a new building, which opened in 1902. Eventually she sold out to James Leys in 1907 and moved to England. The Free Church (left) opened on 27 June 1877 and replaced an earlier church in Constitution Street. Its architect was Mr D. McMillan and it cost £2,987 to build, or £3,183 including the architect's fee.

Shops on West High Street, *c.*1900, illustrating, from left to right, the premises of Sutherland & Son, painters and decorators; Alex J. Smith, watchmaker and jeweller; and William Kemp, newsagent and stationer. Alex Smith inherited the business from his uncle in 1883 having started working in the shop as an apprentice. He was active in the town council as well as various local organisations. From 1874 to 1899 he was deputy town clerk, as well as being clerk at the police court between 1869 and 1886. For over 30 years he was the local correspondent for the *Aberdeen Journal*. He started the local literary society with two friends and was the first secretary of the musical association (established *c.*1876). Additionally he was secretary of the Conservative Association for ten years, and treasurer of both the Savings Bank and Lodge of Freemasons.

The foundation stone of Inverurie Public School was laid in November 1902 at a ceremony performed by the Earl of Kintore, accompanied by his daughter, Lady Ethel Keith-Falconer. Inverurie's new school was designed by A. Marshall Mackenzie of Aberdeen and cost £7,000. The schoolhouse, built at the same time, cost £876. The school had eleven classrooms, each accommodating over 60 pupils, and a central hall measuring 90 feet by 25 feet. Built of grey Aberdeenshire granite ashlar, it was opened in August 1903 by Mr Asher MP, but was badly damaged by fire just three months later. Only one wing remained after the fire. Though it had cost much more than this, the building was only insured for £4,000, but despite the shortfall it was repaired and reopened in January 1905.

Academy and Public School, Inverurie

This picture shows the public school on the right and the academy on the left. The latter was designed by George Gray of Inverurie and was opened on 6 March 1909 by Dr Dunn, Chief Inspector of Schools. It was originally called the Higher Grade School. In 1909 the school leaving age was thirteen and children wishing to go on to secondary education had to travel to Aberdeen (or Fordyce Academy in the case of Alexander Smith) until then. The opening of the academy brought secondary education to children living in Inverurie.

Established in 1845 with its headquarters in Aberdeen, the Great North of Scotland Railway intended to build a line from Aberdeen to Inverness. However it was thwarted by its rivals, the Highland Railway, which also wished to build a route between these two places, and the GNSR only managed to lay tracks between Aberdeen and Elgin. Construction of the section between Inverurie and Huntly began in December 1852, and on 12 September 1854 freight services were introduced between Aberdeen, Inverurie and Huntly. This part of the line was officially opened on 19 September when a special train ran to Huntly. In the 1890s the GNSR made the decision to move its locomotive works from Kittybrewster in Aberdeen to Inverurie. This huge project involved the purchase of nearly 100 acres of land, and in addition to the works themselves houses were built for 112 employees and their families. The total cost was about £100,000. Construction of the workshops began in 1898 and the first buildings were occupied in 1901. The office staff moved in 1903 and the move was completed in 1905 with the arrival of the permanent way department.

In 1902 it was recorded that 'There are at present about 110 persons employed at the new locomotive works, 80 in the carriage and waggon shop, 20 in the paint shop and about 12 temporary hands. In the ensuing May the works will be in full working order, and at least 230 extra workmen will be employed, making a total of about 340. The May contingent will consist chiefly of engineers, blacksmiths and boilermakers' (*The Royal Burgh of Inverurie in the Coronation Year*, p35). The works themselves covered an area of approximately 24 acres, with five blocks of buildings occupying six acres. When they opened Inverurie's population increased by about 1,200. Only ten locomotives were built at the works between 1909 and 1920, partly because of the disruption caused by the First World War during which they were given over to armament production. Following the railway grouping of 1923, when the Scottish companies were taken over by their English counterparts, the building of all new locomotives was moved to sites in England, with Inverurie only undertaking repairs and overhauls from then on. Taken on 13 June 1960, this picture shows class 2P ex-LMS 4-4-0 No. 40661 awaiting attention at Inverurie works.

In addition to building and repairing railway rolling stock, the GNSR pioneered some of the earliest motor bus services in Aberdeenshire in Edwardian times, and the bodies of many of their buses were built at the Inverurie works. Jimmy Brown notes that 'The GNSR had foreseen the development of road transport and were in the vanguard of this new method of transport, running connecting road vehicles from Alford up Donside and from Ballater to Braemar, among other places' (*Inverurie Loco Works, The Inside Story*, p12). This GNSR Milnes–Daimler bus worked the Aberdeen – Skene – Dunecht – Echt service and is seen at the company's shed at Echt *c*.1906.

A second bus built by the GNSR at the Inverurie railway works, also a Milnes–Daimler but of the open charabanc type. The photograph was taken on an excursion at Tillyfourie in 1905 when the vehicle was new. Bodies on these buses could be interchanged for lorry bodies when required. On 31 December 1969 the Inverurie works closed, and the site, buildings and equipment was sold to Aberdeenshire County Council for £25,000.

RAILWAY STATION, INVERURIE

Inverurie's 'new' railway station was opened on 10 February 1902 by William Ferguson, chairman of the GNSR. It replaced an earlier station (with wooden buildings) which had been situated half a mile away, towards Aberdeen at the end of Old Station Road. At the opening ceremony for the new station, William Ferguson was granted the freedom of the burgh, whilst Provost Jackson took the opportunity in his speech to point out that the town council had been petitioning the railway company for a larger and better-appointed station for more than 30 years. The wait seems to have been worthwhile, however, as Mr Jackson was able to conclude that 'now we can congratulate ourselves on possessing the finest and most complete station in the whole kingdom for the size of the place' (*Royal Burgh*, p29).

The section of the main line from Kittybrewster in Aberdeen to Inverurie and Huntly opened to goods traffic on 12 September 1854 and to passengers on 20 September that year. A branch line from Inverurie to Oldmeldrum opened on 26 June 1856, but passenger services were withdrawn on 2 November 1931. Freight traffic used the line until January 1966. This picture shows preserved GNSR locomotive 4-4-0 No. 49 *Gordon Highlander* at Inverurie with a special train for railway enthusiasts on 13 June 1960. Now on display at the Museum of Transport in Glasgow, *Gordon Highlander*, the last surviving GNSR steam engine, was restored to full working order in 1959.

This photograph of a Sentinel steam lorry belonging to Alexander Runcie, carrier, Inverurie, bears a hand-written message on the reverse reading 'Wishing you all a Merry Xmas, 1914'. In addition to running his haulage business, Mr Runcie was also a town councillor. He emigrated to Vancouver with his family in 1929 and died there in November 1941 aged 72 years. The heavily-laden lorry has a stepladder on top (presumably to aid with loading and unloading), and includes amongst its cargo rolls of canvas and an earthenware demijohn contained in a basket. Two of the wooden crates are labelled 'Cadbury's Milk Chocolate' and 'Guaranteed Pure Irish Butter'. The plate on the vehicle's near side reveals that it was a four-ton model.

Proposals for a 'Pleasure Park' were mentioned in the local press in June 1897, and also in September that year when a public park was put forward as one of the suggestions for a permanent memorial to mark Queen Victoria's diamond jubilee of that year. A park had been opened by April 1902 when a Mr J. S. Robertson wrote to the town council requesting permission to play golf there, and included a sketch with proposed holes. After some discussion, permission was granted. 'Councillor Skinner thought he would modify his former opinion, and on seeing the ground, he was satisfied that it would not greatly inconvenience other games' (*Banffshire Journal*, 15 April 1902). Three months later, on 23 July, the golf course was opened by Provost Jackson. 'A large number of members were present, and several enjoyable games were contested' (ibid., 29 July 1902).

Inverurie Parish Church (on the left in this picture) was opened by Revd William Pirie of Dyce on 14 August 1842, replacing an older building said to have been built in 1774 (its manse dated from 1762). The new church was built by George Kemp, a master mason in Inverurie. The minister at the time of its opening, Revd Robert Lessel, had held the post since March 1800, having been a teacher up until that time in Inverurie and elsewhere. When he wrote Inverurie's entry for the *New Statistical Account* the church was still being built, and he recorded that it 'is to contain 1,830 sittings . . . is built of beautiful granite, and is of most substantial workmanship. The style is Gothic, moderately ornamented'. Robert Lessel was succeeded in December 1844 by the Revd John Davidson and died in 1853 aged 95. Revd Davidson was author of *Inverurie and the Earldom of the Garioch*, published in 1878, as well as *Recollections of Forty Years* (1885). In 1929, with the unification of the Parish Church with the Free Church, the building pictured here became the South Church while the Free Church became the West Church. The South Church was renamed St Andrew's Church in 1953.

As a young man, John Annand drove a horse-drawn coach between Inverurie and Aberdeen and was the last owner of the 'Banks of Don' coach. With the opening of the railway line in 1854 and the decline in coaching, he became tenant of the New Inn (at 82 High Street), but soon afterwards transferred to the Kintore Arms Hotel when it opened in 1855. The *Aberdeen Journal* of 11 July that year includes an advert for Annand's Hotel, but it soon became known as the Kintore Arms, which is appropriate as the owner was the Earl of Kintore. Annand was provost of Inverurie from November 1870 until November 1879, and died in 1880 aged 59, leaving a widow, two sons and three daughters. Mrs Annand continued to run the hotel until she retired in 1898, after which it was sold. The purchaser was Alexander D. Hay (of Hay's Soft Drinks) who paid £3,400 for it. The next three owners were George Burnett (1903), A. B. Reid (1905) and R. S. Bryson, who paid about £2,000 for the hotel in 1907.

High Street looking south. By the mid-nineteenth century Inverurie had become a well-established town, with Revd Lessel describing its amenities thus in 1842: 'Branches of the Old Aberdeen Bank, the Town and County Bank, and the North of Scotland Banking Company, have been within a few years established; and among recent improvements ought to be noticed the lighting of the town with gas . . . There is a post-office in the town, and three coaches at least run daily to Aberdeen'. Schooling seems to have advanced in Inverurie too, and in comparison to the single parochial school mentioned in the first *Statistical Account*, Revd Lessel notes that 'Besides the parish school there are five female schools, chiefly for reading English, knitting, and sewing'. The building on the extreme right has been demolished and replaced by a new building set further back from the road occupied by Aberdeenshire Council Social Work Department.

High Street from the air, with the Parish Church in the foreground and a large complex of commercial glasshouses in the centre. Prior to the arrival of large-scale employment (provided principally by the locomotive works) Inverurie was largely a rural community with some cottage industries. In the late eighteenth century William Davidson wrote that 'The women are generally employed in knitting stockings for the Aberdeen manufacturers, and earn from 18 d. to 2 s. a week'. He went on to comment that the town 'does not appear to have ever been a place considerable for trade or manufactures', although this was to change in the future. Ironically, the industrialisation of Aberdeen led to a shortage of local labour in Inverurie: 'Another inconvenience, most sensibly felt of late by the farmers, is a scarcity of servants. Both men and women servants are repairing to Aberdeen, where they readily find employment in the extensive manufactures lately established there, and get high wages. The consequence is, that servants' wages in the country are at least double of what they were a few years ago, and it is difficult to get them at any rate.' (*Statistical Account of Scotland*.)

Inverurie's origins lie in the wooden castle which once stood on the eminence called the Bass, although despite being mentioned in documents dating from 1180 and 1199 little is known about the castle's history. William Davidson described the Bass as 'a curious artificial mount of sand, covered with a fine green sward . . . a truncated cone, very regular, and 40 feet of perpendicular height'. He went on to say that 'The vulgar tradition, about this mount, is a very senseless one. Probably it was a moot-hill, or place where courts were held for administering justice'. Unfortunately he does not enlarge on what the 'vulgar tradition' about its history was! Despite Revd Davidson's assertion, a Geological Survey in 1883 showed that the Bass was not man-made but actually a remarkable natural formation, consisting of many layers of sand in various colours, textures and depths. A church existed for centuries at the Bass until its demolition in 1775.

Inverurie seen from the top of the Bass, *c*.1900, looking toward Beverley Road with the River Ury in the foreground. The Bass rises 50 feet above the river and has a circumference of about 240 feet at the top and 510 feet at its base. Revd Davidson records that Inverurie got its name because of 'its situation at the confluence of the rivers Don and Ury', adding that this location, 'between two such considerable rivers . . . has been a great obstacle to its improvement'. William Hay & Sons owned the post office in Alford as well as a large shop there, and branched out into the manufacture of lemonade in 1884. The business was so successful that they built new premises in Beverley Road, Inverurie, in 1889. While William Hay Jnr. carried on the business in Alford, his younger brother, Alexander D. Hay, moved to Inverurie and ran the business there. In 1881 Alexander married an Inverurie girl, Annie Taylor of 75 High Street, daughter of the postmaster, and later they bought the Kintore Arms Hotel. They had three sons, William, Alexander and Arthur.

The foundation stone of the bridge over the River Don was laid on 27 June 1789 by the 5th Earl of Kintore, and it had been completed by 18 June 1791 when it is mentioned in a letter. The contractor was James Robertson of Banff, and the cost of £2,000 was met by public contributions which had been collected since 1782 when the Earl of Kintore first proposed the idea. The bridge comprised three arches, the middle one being 62 feet wide and the other two 57 feet each in width. Though it appears to have been quite an elegant structure, it had steep approaches and was also very narrow, the roadway being only 16' 3" wide. Tawse and Allen refer to its 'hideous counterforts . . . unevenly shaped and spaced' (p38), and the inadequate bridge was demolished in 1924/5.

The new bridge over the River Don, linking Inverurie with Port Elphinstone, was opened by the 9th Earl of Kintore on 30 May 1925. He was a great-great grandson of the 5th Earl, the man behind the first bridge. In 1922 it was proposed that 'the Town Council should open up negotiations with the County Council with a view to widening of the bridge . . . as motor traffic had become dangerous to public safety' (Tawse, p60). An engineer's report estimated the total cost of a new bridge to be £14,275, of which £2,465 was budgeted for a temporary bridge. Five contractors submitted quotes for the construction work, the lowest of which, £14,983, was supplied by William Tawse of Aberdeen and accepted in March 1924. Work started soon afterwards. With a roadway of 25 feet, plus pavements five feet wide at each side, the new bridge was much wider than its predecessor.

An Edwardian view of Port Elphinstone, with Elphinstone Road in the foreground. Situated on the south side of the River Don, Port Elphinstone was the northern terminus of the Aberdeenshire Canal. This had been surveyed by Thomas Telford in the late eighteenth century and was funded by shareholders mainly consisting of local farmers and gentry. The decision to proceed with the canal was reached in July 1795, but it took more than nine years to construct. Despite officially opening on 31 May 1805, several of the locks had to be rebuilt by the contractor at his own expense and the canal reopened in 1807. It cost £43,895 and measured nineteen miles. Burdened by heavy debts, the canal company was unable to pay any dividends to shareholders until 1840. In 1845 the Aberdeenshire Canal was sold to the Great North of Scotland Railway for £36,000, but only £17,400 was returned to shareholders after debts had been repaid. The GNSR continued to operate the canal until 1852 when it was drained, thereby eliminating a source of competition in the movement of freight and passengers. Afterwards the company made use of its route for a new railway line. In June 1921 Inverurie extended its boundaries to include Port Elphinstone. There was only one house at the port in 1805, but it grew rapidly and had reached a population of 200 by 1852 when the canal closed.

This aerial view shows Port Elphinstone in the foreground and Inverurie in the distance. Passenger services to Aberdeen were provided along the canal and the passenger boats were pulled by a horse with a young rider. It took two and a half hours to reach the terminus at Kittybrewster in Aberdeen, and en route the boats had to negotiate three locks: two at Greenburn near Stoneywood, and another at Haudagain. Goods barges were pulled by two or three horses and took between eleven and fourteen hours to make the journey to Aberdeen harbour, encountering another fourteen locks in the two mile stretch beyond Kittybrewster. The journey involved a total descent of 168 feet with each lock having a drop of ten feet. One local man to make use of the canal, Thomas Tait of Crichie, started a meal mill and sent the oatmeal south in his own boats. In the 1890s Tait's Milling Co. merged with another company to become the North of Scotland Milling Co. Revd Lessel writes in the *New Statistical Account* that 'There are on the canal about thirty barges, besides an iron boat for passengers and light goods, which runs to Aberdeen daily'. Sir Robert Dalrymple Horn Elphinstone (1766–1848) was a shareholder in the canal company and gave his name to Port Elphinstone.

WESTFIELD GARDENS, INVERURIE FROM THE AIR

Inverurie's first council houses were built in 1920 in a new street called Westfield Gardens, seen on the left in this picture, branching off North Street. There were 30 houses in total. The town's population increased with the opening of the Aberdeenshire Canal in 1805, and this growth was consolidated by the subsequent arrival of the railway and large-scale industry (principally the locomotive works). Revd Robert Lessel understood the importance of the canal, writing in 1842 that 'the main cause of the increase and prosperity of Inverury is, without question, the Aberdeen Canal, which has conferred on it many of the advantages of a sea-port'. He went on to add that Port Elphinstone 'exhibits a scene not unlike the quays at Aberdeen, [with] hundreds of carts, sometimes, in a day, delivering grain, and carrying away coals, lime, bones, dung, bricks, iron, timber, or other materials for house-building'.

Inverurie's paper mill was established by Thomas Tait in 1858, soon after the opening of the railway line in 1854. The mill expanded very rapidly and employed 150 people at the time of his death in September 1870. Tait's father was tenant of Crichie Farm and was born there in 1802. Educated at Kintore school and King's College, Aberdeen, Thomas Tait had intended to become a lawyer and joined the firm of Ewen & McHardy, advocates, in Aberdeen. However, when his brother John, who had inherited the farm, died, he came back to Crichie to take it over. Soon after returning he ventured into other businesses, becoming a grain merchant at Port Elphinstone, building his own mill for grinding oats and wheat and making use of the canal to ship the products to Aberdeen harbour. At the time of his death, four of his sons were running the paper mill and a fifth was in charge of the farm. The mill remained in family hands down through his son William (d. 1904), grandson Thomas (d. 1941), great-grandson William (d. 1970) and great-great-grandson Thomas (the present managing director). In 1996 Inverurie Mills became part of the largest paper-making company in the world, International Paper Ltd., and currently employs almost 550 people. Output is approximately 225,000 tons of paper per annum.

In 1662 Sir John Keith bought Caskieben estate in the parish of Monkegy, but soon afterwards changed the name of both the estate and the parish to Keith Hall. According to A. Smith, writing in *A New History of Aberdeenshire*, Sir John built 'the principal part [of Keith Hall], which consists of the front and east wing . . . in 1700'. He was the third son of the 6th Earl Marischal and became the 1st Earl of Kintore in 1667. This honour was bestowed on him by Charles II as a reward for his part in saving the crown jewels of Scotland from falling into English hands at the siege of Dunnottar Castle in 1652. Sir John's part in the affair seems to have been very minor, and involved him sending a letter from France saying that he had arrived there with the crown jewels, thereby deceiving Cromwell's men whilst the jewels were smuggled out of Dunnottar and hidden. The history of Keith Hall (illustrated here) is rather obscure, although it is recorded that 'Sir John built some part of the existing house . . . but how much is uncertain' (Davidson, p 368). In 1985 the building was converted into six houses and eight flats. A later member of the Keith family, Ion Keith-Falconer (younger brother of the 9th Earl) made some notable cycling trips on a penny farthing, including one from Land's End to John O' Groats in June 1882. He covered the distance of 994 miles in twelve days and 23 hours, giving a lecture in the town hall about his memorable feat afterwards.

The Badiefurrow estate was purchased in 1808 by Hugh Gordon, who renamed it Manar. In 1885 the Revd John Davidson wrote that 'The house of Manar . . . was erected by Hugh Gordon after designs by Mr John Smith, architect, Aberdeen; and added to extensively when Manar's [i.e. Gordon's] family were growing up. It occupies the place of a made-up building consisting of the decayed house of Badiefurrow, and an addition needed to make it a habitation when Colonel Erskine Fraser purchased the property [in 1796], and named it Woodhill; which is the original name of a part of the estate that was added to Badiefurrow more than two centuries ago. The house of Badiefurrow . . . had become dilapidated to a great degree, and was for a time occupied by a weaver.' (*Recollections of Forty Years*, p41.) In the *New Statistical Account* of 1842 Revd Robert Lessel describes Manar as being situated three miles west of Inverurie, adding that 'The house is modern, and is at once substantial, comfortable, and commodious'.

KEMNAY. FROM PARKHILL.

220143 J.V.

Though the parish of Kemnay had existed for hundreds of years, Kemnay itself was only a hamlet when the quarry started working in 1858 and the railway station opened in 1859. Before transport and industry arrived it consisted only of the church and manse, a farm called Kirkstyle, a smithy and two or three houses. But Kemnay was transformed very rapidly and by 1871 had a population of about 200 people, this figure rising to nearly 1,000 by 1901. The rapid growth was due to two men, Alexander Burnett and John Fyfe. Burnett, the laird, owned nearly the whole parish including the village and the quarry, while John Fyfe moved his quarrying business to Kemnay in 1858 when he obtained a lease from Burnett on part of Paradise Hill. This view looks across the village towards the quarry, which is visible in the background on the right.

34

MAIN STREET AND U.F. CHURCH, KEMNAY.

Alexander Burnett deserves some credit as the founder of Kemnay village, even though his motive for laying it out was purely to increase his income. The son of John Burnett, he was born in 1816 and inherited Kemnay estate when his father died. He married Letitia Kendall from Gloucestershire and had four children, being widowed in 1855 when he was only 39. With the opening of the quarry (leased to John Fyfe) and the arrival of the railway, Kemnay became a very busy place, but despite this Burnett left Aberdeenshire for the Continent. Prior to doing so he announced his intention to rent out ten acres of land in the village in five areas. These included sections for shops, small villas, and homes for quarry workers, leading to the development of the neat and tidy village seen in this view of Main Street. Burnett's agent rented out property in the village on his boss's behalf, including Kemnay House which was let to Lady Leith for £170 per year.

Kemnay House was built for Sir Thomas Crombie in the seventeenth century, but in 1684 he sold the whole estate to Sir George Nicholson who disposed of it to Thomas Burnett in 1688. His descendant Alexander Burnett (1816–1908) was an absentee landlord for many years, but later returned to spend part of the year in Kemnay, living and travelling in England and the Continent the rest of the time. Incidents in his life included being injured in a railway accident in 1856, and being attacked by a gang in London who 'garrotted and robbed [him] of a fine chronometer watch' (*Aberdeen Journal*, 30 May 1898). His interests included writing to newspapers about religion and his travels. He lost £20,000 (about £2 million at today's values) with the collapse of an Aberdeen company called Blaikies. Locally, Alexander Burnett engaged in many disputes with his tenants. In one instance, in March 1886, 250 tenants marched to protest about what they regarded as the unfair eviction of an industrious tenant, John Milne of Glenhead, who had been told to leave his farm at the end of his nineteen year lease so that the land could be added to the neighbouring farm of Well-leys. Mr Milne had built houses on his farm and had improved the soil fertility, doubling its yield. The tenants marched behind three pipers, carrying an effigy of Mr Burnett which they shot on arriving at Glenhead and burned on their return to the village. A meeting in the village hall decided to send a delegation to Mr Burnett, but its efforts to influence him failed.

Kemnay Pleasure Park opened in 1897 and later incorporated a bowling green and tennis courts. In *Boy in a Village*, Hunter Diack wrote that 'so many quarry workers began to take an interest in bowls that it was decided by everybody concerned to make a regulation size bowling green. This was done by co-operative effort in which the quarriers played a bigger part than anybody. The quoiting club indeed came to an end and bowls became the most popular game in the village' (p138). On the subject of tennis, Diack wrote that 'tennis in Kemnay had a curious history and is linked with the public personality of Weir the chemist . . . He was the leading light in this venture . . . He had support, however, from the new dominie [for the building of tennis courts] . . . There was an elaborate opening ceremony with Mr John Fyfe, the quarry owner, serving the first ball' (ibid. pp 138–9).

Hunter Diack mentions an incident on the Kemnay curling pond in his book *Boy in a Village*: 'Suddenly there was a series of loud cracks. Most of the curling-stones disappeared through the ice, Machray and Rob Duncan, the blacksmith, went with them up to their knees'. Susan Burnett, writing about her grandfather, John Burnett (1852–1935), at Kemnay House, recalls: 'The house is full of cups and trophies that he won . . . He was a very keen and able cricketer and kept wicket for Surrey at one time . . . Later in life he took up curling and became extremely competent and captained the Scottish team for the, then, record number of consecutive wins at Wengen' (Burnett, p211). Kemnay's golf club was established in 1908 and its cricket club *c*.1900.

Andrew Stevenson became the schoolmaster at Kemnay in 1820 and extended the school buildings at his own expense. His school became known as Kemnay Academy and achieved some fame: as well as teaching the local parish boys he also took in boarders, the sons of farmers and country gentlemen (girls were not admitted at the time). There was an orchestra and the school apparently excelled in some artistic areas, but school inspectors decided that his teaching was unsatisfactory.

THE SCHOOL, KEMNAY. A.5491.

Andrew Stevenson died in 1857, almost bankrupt. The two pictures on this page show the new Kemnay Academy (now Kemnay Primary School) which was built in 1874 and extended in 1879 and 1894. Further expansion took place in 1906 when an addition was made to accommodate what was then called the higher grade (i.e. secondary) department.

Although it may look unremarkable, Kemnay's memorial to those who fell in the First World War caused something of a stir in the village, as Hunter Diack recalls: 'It was decided, by whom I do not know, that a fitting memorial would be a German field gun . . . at any rate a German field gun arrived at Kemnay Station . . . [But] the last thing [ex-servicemen] wanted to see in Kemnay . . . was a German field gun. The gun was taken up to a disused quarry-hole called 'the Gullet' and tipped in. It was some time after that that a committee headed by Dr Hendry decided that the sum of £400 which had been raised . . . should be spent on something made of Kemnay granite. There was some talk of a cottage hospital, but there was not enough money for that. I remember seeing various designs passed round [including] an obelisk of Kemnay granite, [which] was the one to be favoured. The conversations I overheard here and there about this memorial gave me the impression that the only person in the village who approved of the design was Dr Hendry himself.' (*That Village on the Don*, pp 110–12.)

This postcard was published by G. Cruickshank of Kemnay and shows the butcher's shop that formed part of the Don Co-operative Society's premises in Aquithie Road. Hunter Diack wrote that 'There were three butcher's shops in the village – Jock Barron's, Alan Reid's and the Don Co-op. Before the war we had sometimes gone to Jock Barron's and sometimes to Alan Reid's, but we registered with Alan Reid. I do not know quite why. His shop was right at the end of Station Road, so we had further to walk. [It] was a solid granite one whereas Jock Barron's was just a large wooden shed, and he looked like a butcher whereas Jock Barron, especially when he was dressed and wearing a bowler, looked like a solicitor' (*That Village on the Don*, p89).

Station Road, Kemnay. The Alford Valley Railway was a branch line running from Kintore to Alford and opened on 21 March 1859 with intermediate stations at Kemnay, Monymusk and Whitehouse. (Another station, at Tillyfourie, opened in 1860.) The *Banffshire Journal* was pleased to note that services on the first day of operation were busy, reporting that 'there was a good commencement, eighty passengers going up with the first two trains, besides fifteen waggon-loads of goods, mostly manures from Aberdeen' (22 March 1859). The first station at Kemnay was described as 'a neat little thing', and was probably made of wood; it was situated behind what is now Alldays store and 'the entrance gate was immediately opposite the lane beside the Laird's Throat Public House' (Downie, p11). When the railway arrived, Kemnay was just a hamlet and could not be seen from the railway line because of a ridge.

Kemnay's inhabitants were opposed to the station being moved to a new site, and held a public meeting to protest about it in March 1898. A month later, a deputation met with directors of the Great North of Scotland Railway to urge that the station should be kept in its original location, but without any success.

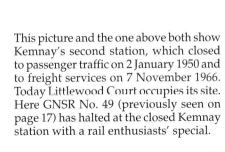

This picture and the one above both show Kemnay's second station, which closed to passenger traffic on 2 January 1950 and to freight services on 7 November 1966. Today Littlewood Court occupies its site. Here GNSR No. 49 (previously seen on page 17) has halted at the closed Kemnay station with a rail enthusiasts' special.

The Burnett Arms Hotel, which bears the date 1902, was popular with anglers (who still call in for refreshments today) and once had fishing rights on the River Don. In the first *Statistical Account* for the Parish of Kemnay, the Revd Patrick Mitchell wrote: 'The Don, which is our only river, abounds in excellent salmon. The way in which they are caught here is by cruives, of which there are two belonging to Mr Burnett of Kemnay. The salmon are sent fresh to Aberdeen for exportation, and are sold to the merchant at 4 d. the pound, from the beginning of the fishing season to the middle of April, and thence, to the end of the season, at 3½ d. the pound.' The picture was more gloomy when the Revd George Peter wrote Kemnay's entry for the *New Statistical Account* in the 1840s: 'The [Don] used to abound throughout in excellent salmon. A very great proportion is now intercepted by the stake-nets and cruives at and near the mouth of the river.' A cruive is a fish trap formed from a row or enclosure of closely placed stakes.

Kemnay Public Hall opened on 7 November 1878 and cost £498. The architect was a Mr Gillie. At the opening, John Charles of Inverurie alluded in his speech to the principal source of Kemnay's growth and prosperity – the quarry and the man behind it, John Fyfe, noting that 'it was owing to his pluck, energy and perseverance, that Kemnay was now what it was' (*Banffshire Journal*, 12 November 1878). John Charles was agent for the Town and County Bank in Inverurie. He later became a JP and from 1895 was provost of Inverurie.

Kendall Road, Kemnay. Revd Patrick Mitchell described Kemnay's occupants thus in the first *Statistical Account*: 'There are 4 weavers, 3 tailors, 1 blacksmith, 3 shoemakers, 2 joiners, and 1 cartwright. . . . There are also 2 grocers, one of whom is a distiller. . . . The women never work in the fields but in harvest. They are constantly employed in household affairs, and in knitting coarse worsted stockings for exportation, which is the only manufacture which has been introduced into the district. The Aberdeen hosiers take in the manufactured stockings, and give out wool once a month. . . . Several of the men, when they become old, and unfit for working in the fields, employ themselves in spinning and knitting.'

Though quarrying at Kemnay had begun in the 1830s, the industry only developed rapidly after the quarry was leased by John Fyfe in 1858. Fyfe was an experienced quarryman who already owned the Tyrebagger quarry near Aberdeen, which he had inherited from his father in 1846 at the age of sixteen. Kemnay's grey granite was used in many buildings, with notable examples including Marischal College (the largest granite building in the world after the Escorial in Spain) and His Majesty's Theatre in Aberdeen, and the Cenotaph in London. There was also a huge market for causeway (cassie) blocks, also known as cobbles or setts, for city streets. The grandfather of Hunter Diack, who wrote two books about life in Kemnay, was one of the first foreman-managers at the quarry.

This postcard is captioned 'Mason's Sheds, Kemnay Quarries' and shows a partially-completed item of work in the centre of the picture with cranes on tracks either side of it. The cable above the cranes, attached to the pylon-type structure on the right, formed part of the Blondin or aerial lifting gear which was used to lift large blocks of granite out of the quarry. This was named after Charles Blondin (1824–97), a Frenchman who crossed the Niagara Falls on a tightrope, later repeating the feat blindfold and then pushing a wheelbarrow. The Blondin was one of a number of quarrying innovations introduced by John Fyfe and was first used at Kemnay in 1873. It allowed stone to be lifted out of the quarry from greater depths than previously. Fyfe was inspired to install it having seen mail being carried across the River Dee at Abergeldie Castle using a similar aerial system. In conjunction with a young engineer called Andrew Barclay, John Fyfe developed a steam crane which was 'first introduced at Kemnay and went on to revolutionise quarrying' (*John Fyfe, One Hundred and Fifty Years*). Over 300 men were employed at Kemnay quarry, including 160 sett-makers. Others worked as masons, crane-drivers, Blondin drivers, joiners, blacksmiths, engineers and 'firemen'. The latter carried out blasting operations, a dangerous task which sometimes resulted in horrific accidents in which men were crushed to death by huge slabs of rock.

In the blacksmith's shop at Kemnay quarry. John Fyfe was born at Bucksburn, Aberdeen in 1830 and in 1868 married Barbara Stevenson, daughter of a grocer from Dalmadilly, Kemnay. The couple had two sons and eight daughters. Other quarries opened by Fyfe included Tom's Forest (Kintore), Tillyfourie and Corrennie. After John Fyfe's death in 1906 his son, John M. Fyfe, became managing director of the quarrying empire. One of the company's biggest contracts was to supply stone for the Thames Embankment, a project which is said to have kept 500 masons in work for seven years. Finished blocks of granite were transported to London in Fyfe's own ships, the *Black Dwarf* and the *White Witch*. An Act of Parliament of 1862 authorised the building of the embankment, specifying its length as 5,710 feet and awarding contracts totalling approximately £750,000 for the work. This major civil engineering project extended from Westminster to Blackfriars Bridges.